Quick Reference Herbal Guide

for Cats and Dogs

By

C.D. Meacham, Master Herbalist

ISBN: 978-0-557-69576-8

Please visit www.herbalcindy.com for more information.

Cover art by S. Margaret Meacham

Disclaimer—The information in this book is in no way meant to be a substitute for professional veterinary care. You alone, as a responsible care-giver, must decide when it is prudent to seek professional veterinary care for your companion animal.

Note-- Please read all of the information provided in the first part of this book to familiarize yourself with the techniques of herbal medicine before you need them. Foreknowledge will help you be better prepared for emergencies.

Warning—This book is divided into separate sections for cats and dogs for a serious reason. DO NOT USE THE DOG REMEDIES LISTED IN THIS BOOK ON A CAT. ALTHOUGH SAFE FOR A DOG, SOME OF THE REMEDIES LISTED HERE ARE NOT SAFE FOR A CAT.

Table of Contents

What Makes This Book Different?

In a very direct sense, I wrote this book for myself. During the many years I studied to become a Master Herbalist, I would spend hours poring over several different books to find just the right herbal remedy for each particular ailment for whatever I was helping—a cat with a bladder infection, a Dachshund with Parvo, a chicken under severe stress, a toddler with allergies, a new mother, a man with arthritis, a grandmother with osteoporosis, a puppy with..., etc.

But I don't like to rely on memory alone when it comes to anyone's health. Since I hate repeating myself, I wrote down the results of each research session to avoid having to look through the same twelve books again, eight months later. In the end, my notes turned out to be extensive enough to become a book of their own. So here it is. However, this book is by no means exhaustive.

No one book will give you all the answers in a page or two. This book probably won't give you all the answers either, but it's a quick place to start. If you want to know more about a particular topic, check out the recommended reading list in the back of this book. However, be aware that most books won't give you information on possible adverse reactions or possible side effects. Nor will they necessarily indicate the safe use of an herb for a specific species. I have tried to cover both of these issues in this book.

If you do decide to do additional research, be aware that herbs can affect cats, dogs, or people in severely different ways. Cats can be especially difficult to help because a cat can die from a remedy that's safe to give to a dog of the same size.

DO NOT USE THE DOG REMEDIES LISTED IN THIS BOOK ON A CAT. YOU COULD KILL YOUR CAT IF YOU DO.

Also, this book is deliberately meant to be simple. I know of many remedies that require several different, and often hard

to find, ingredients. Many authors will tell you that all of these many ingredients are needed because herbs work synergistically, that is to say they work better in combination than when used alone. Although this is often true, it's not a hard and fast rule. I've often achieved excellent results with one herb instead of four. If I need to use a more complicated remedy to help, I will, but I don't like to start out that way. I prefer to use what helps the most, one herb at a time.

Again, please read all of the information provided in the front, or "How To" part of this book to familiarize yourself with the techniques of herbal medicine before you need them. Foreknowledge will help you be better prepared for emergencies.

I sincerely hope the information in this book will help your cats and dogs live long, healthy and happy lives with you.

C.D. Meacham

The Importance of Diet

As with humans, nutrition is the cornerstone of holistic health. For us, a healthy diet should include vegetables, grains, nuts, fish, fowl, and limited amounts of red meat, dairy and processed (white) sugar. In a perfect world our food should come from unpolluted, organic sources that have the perfect balance of minerals, i.e. from land that hasn't been over farmed.

There is a debate among holistic animal practitioners as to what the "Perfect" diet for a pet should be. Some say that since the prey of cats and dogs often have vegetables in their stomach when they are killed, that our cats and dogs should follow basically the same diet we humans do: the veggies, the grains, the meat and eggs.

Some practitioners say they should only be given cooked meats, while others say they should only eat raw meats.

Then some vegetarians give their carnivorous pets only vegetables. I personally believe this to be a huge mistake. Carnivores are meant to eat meat. It's okay to feed them vegetables occasional-

ly, but they are designed to eat meat. I've read of many dogs dying of starvation because their vegetarian masters refused to feed them meat. If meat is against your beliefs, I strongly urge you to consider keeping an herbivore for a pet instead of a cat or dog. This situation is similar to having to feed a snake live food. If you don't want to feed the animal what it needs to be healthy, than please don't keep the animal for a pet. We have to love animals for what they are, not what we want them to be. Please do some research into what the animal needs before obtaining one.

In my opinion most commercial food, canned or dry, is not good for our pets. It's marketed to get your attention, not to prolong the health and wellbeing of your companion.

It's best to give your pet the most natural source of food, and non-chlorinated water she will tolerate. Fruits and veggies for herbivores; meat and bone for carnivores. Interestingly, flesh will make any animal gain weight while bone won't. Also, raw bones are more pliable than cooked bones. Avoid giving a dog/cat cooked fowl (chicken) bones. Once

cooked, the bones of a bird become brittle and can catch in the animal's throat. Your companion could choke to death. This does not hold true for pork or beef bones. It's okay to give your companion cooked pork or beef bones.

In addition to flesh and bone, your companion cat will also need regular servings of organ meats, especially heart meat. Heart meat contains a digestive enzyme which a cat's body does not produce on its own. Without this enzyme a cat will eventually die. Chicken hearts are the best source known for this enzyme. Organ meats are also an excellent source of essential fatty acids, which help keep cats and dogs healthy.

If you decide to feed your companion a natural diet, be sure to keep the chunks of food a reasonable size for a cat or smaller dog to chew. Bigger animals can handle bigger chunks.

However, keep in mind that the highest quality natural food won't do Fido any good if he won't eat it. Case in point—My dog Charlie does just fine on raw bone as his main source of food. On the other hand, my cat Jimmie wouldn't even lick

raw meat or drink bottled water. I suppose he needed the minerals in tap water.

If your pet is a "kibble or die" type, try switching him to a natural brand of kibble, like Nutro Natural Choice. You'll want to find a kibble high in essential fatty acids, or EFA's. Even a small change can make a big difference. I once helped an older dog who was dying of liver failure. Just by changing to a natural kibble, her human was able to extend her life, and her quality of life, for several months.

But beware—just because the label says "All Natural" doesn't mean the food is actually good for your pet.

Avoid high fructose corn syrup and "All natural by-products"

For cats you might want to avoid citric acid—Cats tend to store toxins in their livers and they don't process any type of citrus.

If you have a large or giant breed dog you'll want to avoid commercial foods altogether. A link has been established between cancer in larger breed dogs, and some commercial dry dog foods.

However, Fluffy's diet also has to be something you can live with. I've read book after book of stories where people 'cook' especially for their dogs and cats every week and store the food in containers. That's not something I want to do for my dogs at this point in my life. I love my dogs dearly. I just don't want to cook for them. However, I did cook for Jimmie, my tabby cat, when he fought his battle with cancer and diabetes. With the help of diet and herbs we were able to extend his quality of life for more than a year.

My biggest test subject for herbalism and animals is Charlie. We (my family) got him from Az Pyrs., the rescue group for Great Pyrenees dogs in Arizona, specifically because he had serious health issues and I knew I could help him with herbs. When he came to rescue his belly was red, raw and bald, and he had severe allergies to all the commercial foods. He weighed only 103 when we got him, which was very thin for a dog of his height and breed. He had constant ear infections, and he was scared to death of cats. He also had severe fear of being hand fed, because he had been teased with and then beaten over table food. It took us about 1½ years to iron out his physical health issues, and another 1½ to bring healing to his emotional health. Now he's fine with cats. But he hates the puppy.

The first step to wellness for Charlie was to get him on the BARF diet—Biologically Appropriate Raw Food. For Charlie that meant 1 ½ pounds of raw chicken frames and a cup of minced, raw vegetables with a tablespoon of olive oil a day. However, that changed in a hurry. He got tired of the chicken and he wouldn't touch his veggies after about a week. So we switched him to raw pork necks and he loves leftovers from dinner—especially split pea soup, bread and pumpkin pie. However, avoid giving your companion sweets if she has an ear infection. The sugar might make the infection worse, especially if it's a yeast infection.

Although we in my family are open to giving our dogs table food, we don't give our pets chocolate. It contains the chemical theobromine, which has been known to cause seizures, damage heart tissue, and cause internal bleeding of the intestinal tract in dogs. Some people

feed their dogs chocolate and the dog's just fine. It all depends on the dog's tolerance for the chemical. You might be able to feed your companion small amounts of chocolate for months and then, suddenly there can be a big, expensive problem.

We've also stopped giving our dogs cookies with raisins in them, because it's recently been found that raisins can induce renal failure in dogs.

Note: Citrus oils, (orange, lemon, grapefruit, etc,) garlic, onions and lilies are toxic to cats. Although you may find some references which recommend garlic as an immune booster for cats, I don't think it's a good idea to even use it topically because of how cats groom themselves. I think it may be an issue of tolerance in the cat's body, as chocolate is for a dog, but I wouldn't want to take the chance unless directed by a holistic vet.

In a perfect world we've all had our fur babies since they were born. We've fed them a perfect BARF diet since they were weaned and they are in absolutely perfect health. Unfortunately, life doesn't work that way. Even if you do everything

right to give your companion a good, healthy diet, many specific breeds are prone to specific ailments. For example, Boston Terriers are prone to seizures because their skulls are too small for their brains, and Great Danes are prone to heart failure. Here's where herbs can make a big, positive difference in the quality of life for your companions. Seizures can be controlled with the herb Skull Cap, and heart function can be improved with Hawthorn.

In Charlie's case, about 80% of his health problems went away by changing to a natural diet. The rest of his physical problems went away with herbal supplements.

About Herbs

Herbs are usually sold in dried, encapsulated form. Dried herbs have a longer shelf life. When giving herbs to a companion animal, it's okay to open the capsule up and add the herb to food. Butter or potted meat often works well when dosing the tamest of animals.

Keep in mind that most of the dosages listed on the bottles of herbal supplements are meant for people who weigh 150 pounds. That means, if the dosage calls for two capsules, a person or animal weighting 75 pounds needs only one capsule. For those weighing less, only part of the capsule is needed. For a 10 pound cat or dog just a pinch will do.

If your dog is big enough, say the size of a 100 pound woman, it's okay to simply push capsules down his throat. Be sure to push the dog's upper lip over one of his canine teeth as you gently pry his mouth open with one hand and push the capsule(s) down his throat with the other. Folding his lip over his tooth, like

that, will prevent him from biting you. Because dogs have short digestive tracts, capsules aren't necessarily the most effective way to administer herbs to them, but capsules can be the easiest way to get herbs into your dog, if she is large.

Medicinal Teas

Medicinal teas often work well as eye or ear washes.

<u>How to Make Medicinal Teas</u>: Depending on the part of the plant you need to use, there are 2 ways to make a medicinal tea. If you need to use the leaf or flower, bring one pint of filtered water to a boil. Take off of the heat and add two tea bags, or one tablespoon of the dried herb to the water. Let steep for 10 minutes. Allow to cool. Be sure to strain the tea through a coffee filter to remove all particles from the liquid if you're making an eye or ear wash.

If you're using the root of a plant, add two tea bags or one tablespoon of the fresh or dried herb to a pint of filtered water and bring to a boil over medium heat. Let stand for at least 10 minutes. Then strain. Remember to use a coffee filter if you're making an eye or ear wash.

Tinctures

Tinctures are liquid herbal extracts in an alcohol or glycerin base. Although a tincture based in alcohol is the best quality tincture available, consider why you need it before choosing the type of base in which it's made. If you need to use a tincture to treat a wound or sore, you definitely want to use a glycerin based tincture to avoid making the wound burn in addition to hurting.

Because they allow you to adjust the dosage precisely, tinctures are a very effective way to administer herbs to an animal, especially a small one. Although some books will tell you it's okay to give a few drops of tincture to a companion straight from the bottle, this is a bad idea. I tried it on myself and it took 3 days for the burn under my tongue to go away. As with people, it's best to dilute the tincture in water first.

Keep in mind that like most herbal products, the recommended dosage listed on the bottle of tincture is usually meant for a person weighing 150 pounds. If your companion weighs only 10 pounds you'll need to reduce the amount of tincture you give to her. In an instance where you would give a person 30 drops, you'll only have to give your 10 pound cat 2 drops of the same tincture.

How to Dilute a Tincture for a Dog or Cat: You'll need a 1 oz dropper bottle filled to the shoulder with filtered water. (Tap water will work too, if that's all you have available.) If the instructions on the bottle of tincture say, "Add 30 to 40 drops to an ounce of water," you'll need to cut the dosage down to 1 drop of tincture in the bottle per every 5 pounds of your companion's weight. Then give your companion one dropper full of the diluted tincture as many times a day as directed. If your fur-baby needs more than one tincture at a time, it's okay to add two or

three tinctures to the same dropper bottle of water, but a single dose is still one dropper full at a time.

If the recommended number of drops is different than the above example, be sure to keep the proportion of drops to weight the same. For example, if the bottle recommends only 15 drops for an adult's dosage, you'd only have to add one drop of tincture to the ounce of water to make the appropriate dilution. When in doubt always use a lower dosage for your companion.

If per chance you already have some glycerin based tincture on hand when Fido needs a dose internally, it's okay to give him what you have, but be sure to dilute it as indicated above.

Over Dose

If you accidently give your companion too much of an herb he'll either vomit it up or have diarrhea for a short while. Although this would add to your companion's discomfort, it shouldn't last for more than a few hours. The same holds true for people.

Allergic Reaction

Although allergic reaction is uncommon, it is always possible. When in doubt, go slow. It's often wise to start your companion off with a lower dose of whatever and watch them for any odd behaviors, i.e. lethargy, dizziness, scratching, vomiting, diarrhea, or rash. Again, the same holds true for people.

Bach Flower Remedies

Anyone who truly pays attention to the animals they live with knows that animals have feelings. I've seen it myself. I know cats and dogs worry, suffer depression and grieve. I also know it's sometimes difficult to live with an animal that has been emotionally damaged. That's why I tend to get my dogs from rescue. I know I can help them heal physically, if needed, and emotionally. To speed up the process of emotional healing, I use Bach Flower Remedies (BFR's).

Developed by Dr. Edward Bach, this system is based on 38 remedies which seek to heal a person's, or animal's, emotional state. As many others before and since him, Dr. Bach believed in a connection between the mind and body. Both need to be in balance for complete wellness of the person or animal.

Although they are related to homeopathic remedies, BFR's are more gentle and safer. Yet, they are very effective. The biggest trick with them is choosing the one(s) you need. The nicest thing about them is they are very safe to use. You can't OD on them. Nor do they con-

flict with prescription medications. And if you give your companion "the wrong one" it won't affect, or hurt him in any way. If you give him the one(s) he needs, you should notice a positive change in his behavior in less than 2 weeks. The same holds true for people.

Bach Flower Remedies are readily available at many health food-grocery stores, but they need to be diluted before use. Simply add two drops of remedy to a one ounce bottle of filtered water. Then dose from the diluted bottle. Considering that you probably won't need even half of the remedy you purchase in one bottle, it's usually cheaper to buy a prepared remedy from a BFR practitioner, such as myself.

Common Ailments & Problems in Dogs

Note: If at all possible, try to improve your companion's diet first. Herbal remedies are meant to augment a healthy life style, not just compensate for bad habits.

Allergies

As with people, most of an animal's immunity to illness comes from the digestive system. Allergies are considered a dysfunction of the immune system. What you want to do is calm the immune system down and improve your companion's digestion. Obviously, if you know what your companion is allergic to, try to help your pet avoid it. Then try to put your pet on as natural a diet as she/he will tolerate. Next you'll want to supplement that diet with Acidophilus—a probiotic that helps carnivores digest proteins. You may also want give your pet some essential fatty acids daily. The best source is fish oil, but avoid using a source that has lemon added to it, if you have a cat. Lemon oil will kill a cat. Olive oil will also work.

If your companion is allergic to grass, consider administering nettle tincture once or twice daily.

See page 16 for instructions on how to dilute tinctures.

Arthritis

From a holistic standpoint, arthritis is considered an auto-immune disease. The first thing you'll want to consider is to put your companion on as natural (raw) a diet as they will tolerate. This is sometimes difficult. As with allergies, what you want to do is calm the immune system down and improve your companion's digestion.

Next you'll want to supplement that diet with Acidophilus—a probiotic that helps carnivores digest proteins. You may also want give your pet some essential fatty acids daily. The best source is fish oil, but avoid giving your cat a source that has lemon added to it. Lemon oil will kill a cat.

Any other herbal supplements you wish to consider for your companion will depend on his medical history. You'll also want to consider administering something for his pain. See page 37 for information on pain relief.

Asthma & Bronchitis

Consider administering Mullein tincture 2 to 3 times daily.

See page 16 for instructions on how to dilute tinctures.

If something stronger is needed, consider trying a product called ALJ which is produced by Nature's Sunshine Products. This liquid herbal extract is composed of Boneset, Fenugreek seeds, Horseradish root, Mullein leaves and Fennel seed and is very effective for alleviating breathing problems.

You'll need to dilute it in water as you would dilute a tincture. Be sure to keep the proportion of drops to weight the same as you would for an adult weighing 150 pounds. For this remedy you'll want

to give your dog no more than 1 drop for every 5 pounds of dog Then give her one dropper full of the dilution at a time.

Steam is also good for lung problems. Consider having your companion in the bathroom with you when you take a shower.

Barking Excessively

Excessive barking is often an emotional issue for a dog. Consider administering a Bach Flower Remedy such as Chicory or Heather. The specific remedy needed depends on what's going on with your dog. See the recommended reading list for an excellent book on Bach Flower Remedies or contact me.

Bite or Puncture Wound

The goal here is to flush germs and any foreign materials out of the wound before it becomes infected. Squeeze sterile saline nasal spray over and into the wound

in order to wash it out as much as possible. Follow with an application of non-alcohol based herbal tincture of Oregon Grape, Golden Seal or Echinacea. You may have to do this a few times a day for a few days to keep the wound clean until it heals over. If there are no signs of improvement or you notice swelling around the bite, consider a trip to the vet.

DO NOT USE POWERED TURKEY RHUBARB ON A DEEP WOUND. IT COULD CAUSE THE WOUND TO FESTER.

Bladder Infection

First, try changing to a holistic diet. Often this is sufficient to clear up the infection. If changing the diet doesn't work, consider administering cranberry tincture, 3 to 4 times daily, for a few days. If the infection persists for more than 10 days, consider taking Fluffy to the vet.

Caution: Don't give your companion cranberry tincture if you know she has a kidney problem.

See page 16 for instructions on how to dilute tinctures.

Bleeding of a Small Wound or Cut.

On a clean wound and with clean hands, sprinkle a generous amount of powered Turkey Rhubarb over the wound. It will stick to the wound by itself. Leave it in place. If the powder gets washed out of the wound/cut it will start bleeding again. The powder will wear away as the wound heals. It shouldn't be necessary to apply a bandage unless your companion licks the wound too much to let the powder work.

Burns, Minor Only

Bathe the burn immediately with lots of cool water. Then apply Aloe Vera gel to the affected area. Avoid using too much Aloe Vera for too long. It might give your companion diarrhea.

Cancer

This is a very serious situation for both you and your companion. You as the caregiver have some very difficult decisions to make. Allopathic treatment for cancer is often very expensive and traumatic for the entire family. However, holistic alternatives do exist.

After you've both come home from the vet, the first thing you'll want to consider is putting your companion on as natural (raw) a diet as she will tolerate. This is sometimes difficult but worth a try or two. Also consider administering Cat's Claw tincture, 3 to 4 times daily. See page 16 for instructions on how to dilute tinctures.

Also check the internet for info on holistic cancer treatments for your companion. What you'll need depends on the type of cancer your pet has.

If you decide to put your companion to sleep, that's okay too. The decision is yours.

Constipation

Try giving your companion a teaspoonful of fish oil in their food. For bigger dogs try a tablespoon full. DO NOT GIVE YOUR CAT FISH OIL WITH LEMON ADDED. Lemon oil will kill a cat.

You might alternatively use olive oil or butter

Cough

What one uses to alleviate a cough, depends on why your companion has a cough.

If the cough is related to asthma, bronchitis or a cold, try Mullein tincture 2 to 3 times daily.

If something stronger is needed, Nature's Sunshine Products produces ALJ, a liquid herbal extract composed of Boneset, Fenugreek seeds, Horseradish root, Mullein leaves and Fennel seed, which is very effective for breathing problems.

Steam is also good for lung problems. As with asthma, try keeping your companion in the bathroom with you when you take a shower. The steam should help.

If your companion's cough is related to cancer, consider administering Cat's Claw tincture.

See page 16 for instructions on how to dilute tinctures.

Diabetes

If you decided against allopathic treatment for your companion, consider administering Dandelion tincture once or twice daily.

Diarrhea

Consider adding some powered Slippery Elm to food. If the stool is bloody try administering Yarrow tincture in addition to Slippery Elm. One or two doses of Yarrow are often sufficient. The probiotic, Acidophilus, is helpful too. If the diarrhea lasts for more than a week, or

gets worse, consider a trip to the vet. For very small dogs and puppies, consider a trip to the vet if the remedy doesn't work in 24 hours.

Ear Infection

According to my experience, dogs are more prone to ear infections than cats. However, I've found a simple remedy that's appropriate for both. Nature's Sunshine Products makes a liquid herbal remedy called CBG Extract. Its contents include Chickweed, Black Cohosh and Golden Seal. If you're in a hurry, you can use it on your companion or yourself, straight from the bottle. Simply shake, drip a drop or two into the effected ear and massage for a while. Sometimes one dose is enough to clear up the problem. But since it comes in an alcohol base, avoid using it straight from the bottle if the ear in question is sore or raw.

Ear Pain Drops for Dogs

To a 1 oz dropper bottle add

1 tablespoon CBG Extract

1 tablespoon olive oil

2-3 droppers full of non-alcohol based Mullein Extract

1 capsule of garlic oil—puncture with a knife and squeeze the oil into the bottle

DO NOT ADD GARLIC OIL IF THE DROPS ARE FOR A CAT.

Shake well. Add a drop or 2 into the affected ear and massage.

You'll also want irrigate your companion's ears with ear wash once or twice a week until the infection clears up. If it doesn't clear up within 2 weeks, consider a trip to the vet.

Ear Infection, Chronic

If your companion suffers from chronic ear infections, the first thing you'll want to do is switch him to as natural diet as

possible. If you've already done that and he's still having ear infections, the next thing you'll want to try is administering essential fatty acids daily. The best source is fish oil, but <u>avoid using a source that has lemon added to it, if you have a cat. Lemon oil will kill a cat.</u>

Also consider irrigating his ears with ear wash on a regular basis.

<u>To make ear wash</u>: First, make Bergamot tea: Bring one cup of filtered water to a boil. Take off of the heat and add a Bergamot tea bag. Let steep for 10 minutes. Allow to cool. Strain through a coffee filter to remove all particles from the liquid. For a small dog (10 to 30 pounds), pour a dropper full of ear wash into each ear and rub the ear gently. Then let the dog shake his/her head. The ear wash should help dislodge any dirt or earwax from the ear. The ear wash will also help clean bacteria and other microbes out of the ear and help your dog avoid ear infections.

For larger dogs, use an ear bulb full for each ear, rub the ears gently and let the dog shake his/her head.

As with other remedies, be sure to use the ear wash at room temperature. It's okay to warm the bottle under hot running water if you've stored it in the refrigerator, but don't get the drops too hot. Test them on your wrist, as you would a baby's bottle. Unrefrigerated, the wash should last 7 to 10 days. If refrigerated the ear wash should store safely for up to 6 months.

Eye Irritation- If your companion gets something in her eyes, a quick way to help is to flush out her eyes with an herbal wash. Our dog Tatum once got into an ant's nest. The eye wash listed below cleared up her problem in one day.

To make eye wash: Prepare Raspberry leaf tea: Bring one cup of filtered water to a boil. Take off of the heat and add a

raspberry leaf tea bag. Let steep for 10 minutes. Allow to cool. Strain through a coffee filter to remove all particles from the liquid. Then pour 1 ounce of sterile saline solution into a clean container. Add ½ teaspoon of cooled and strained Raspberry leaf tea. (Tea made from the fruit of raspberries won't work.) Shake gently to distribute the tea throughout the saline solution. Pour into a 1 oz dropper bottle and apply a drop or two in the affected eye twice daily for a few days. The eyewash may work in only one application.

As always, be sure to use the drops at room temperature. It's okay to warm the bottle up under hot running water if you've stored it in the refrigerator, but don't get the drops too hot. Test them on your wrist, as you would a baby's bottle.

If the irritation persists for more than a few days, consider taking your dog to the vet.

Unrefrigerated, the drops should last 7 to 10 days. If refrigerated the eyewash

should store safely for up to 6 months.

Note: Go ahead and drink the rest of the raspberry tea, if you wish. You probably won't need to make more than one bottle of eyewash to help your dog.

Fur Ball

Try a tablespoonful of olive oil. Butter may also be helpful.

Gingivitis

First, try getting your companion to eat a natural diet, including raw bones. If that doesn't work, try dipping a cotton swap in non-alcohol based Golden Seal tincture and gently rub the swap across the involved gums. Don't use Golden Seal for more than 10 days straight. It can have a negative impact on your companion's digestive system.

Heart Failure, Congestive

If you decide against allopathic treatment for your companion, try administering a tincture of Hawthorne, which includes the leaf and berry.

See page 16 for instructions on how to dilute tinctures.

Pain

For dogs larger than 35 pounds it's okay to administer Ascriptin. This over-the-counter pain reliever is a blend of aspirin and Maalox. Each tablet is meant for a person or dog weighing 75 pounds.
A dog weighing 35 to 70 pounds should be given ½ a tablet up to 3 times daily.
A dog weighting 75 to 90 pounds can be given 1 whole tablet up to 3 times daily.
A giant breed dog weighing 90+ pounds can be given 2 whole tablets up to 3 times daily. Administer the Ascriptin at

least 4 hours apart as needed.
Warning for Cats: DO NOT GIVE ASCRIPTIN TO A CAT. IT WILL DIE IF YOU DO.

Warning for Dogs: DO NOT USE ASCRIPTIN ON A DOG WEIGHING LESS THAN 35 POUNDS. IT'S TOO DIFFICULT TO GET THE DOSAGE LOW ENOUGH.
DO NOT GIVE ASCRIPTIN TO A DOG WHO IS BLEEDING OR HAS BLOODY STOOL.
IT WILL MAKE THE BLEEDING WORSE.

DO NOT GIVE REGULAR ASPIRIN TO A DOG. IT WILL CAUSE STOMACH UPSET.

Parvo

Parvo is a virus that causes diarrhea so severe that the dog ends up voiding the lining of its own intestines. Consider administering Cat's Claw tincture, an anti-viral agent, and Yarrow, to help stop the bleeding. Take your dog to the vet as soon as possible. Dog's can die of this disease in a matter of hours, and it is very contagious among dogs.

See page 16 for instructions on how to dilute tinctures.

Poisoning

If you suspect your companion has been exposed to a poison, and is still conscious, try administering Milk Thistle tincture as soon as possible and go to the vet. I've had good success in mixing the tincture in a glob of butter and forcing it into the animal's mouth.

See page 16 for instructions on how to dilute tinctures.

Use butter instead of water in this instance.

Seizures

If you decide against allopathic treatment for your companion, try administering Skullcap tincture 2 to 3 times daily. If the seizures don't stop completely, try adding Valerian tincture to the dilution.

See page 16 for instructions on how to dilute tinctures.

Stress relief

Administer 2 drops or one dropper full of diluted Rescue Remedy under your dogs tongue. Rescue Remedy is very effective for relief of emotional upset and/or minor pain. It will help keep your dog calm if administered prior to visiting the vet and prior to grooming. It will also help comfort the dying.

Rescue Remedy also comes in an alcohol-free formula, which can be administered directly from the bottle.

Trauma, Severe

If your dog is unlucky enough to get hit by a car, or suffers some other severe, life threatening injury you need to get him to a vet as soon as possible. While in transit you'll want to gently rub the tip of one of his ears. I know this sounds off beat. However, the ear is a life energy point used in the TTellington Touch system.

Recommended Supplies to Have Available In Case of Emergencies for Your Dog

Included in kit for Dogs Available

from HerbalCindy.com

One emergency muzzle—to make sure you don't get bitten while you're trying to ease your dog's suffering. Put it around your dog's muzzle before you start working on him/her. Even the tamest of dogs may end up biting you if he/she is in pain.

Lavender Water 1% Dilution—for relief of itching, skin irritation & rash. Shake well and spray the affected area, 2 to three times daily. Will also help calm your dog when sprayed around the room. Use sparingly.

Alcohol-Free Rescue Remedy—for relief of emotional upset and/or minor pain.

Administer 2 drops or one dropper full

of diluted Rescue Remedy under your dogs tongue.

Alcohol-Free Rescue Remedy can be administered directly from the bottle if necessary.

1 (5 count) Package of Slippery Elm Capsules—to help relieve diarrhea. Each capsule is meant for a person or dog weighing 75 pounds.

A dog weighing less than 35 pounds can be given a sprinkle of the herb, in food, once or twice daily as needed.

A dog weighing 35 to 70 pounds can be given ½ a capsule once or twice daily as needed.

A dog weighing 75 to 90 pounds can be given 1 whole capsule once or twice daily as needed.

A giant breed dog weighing 90+ pounds can be given 2 whole capsules once or twice daily as needed.

Sterile Saline Nasal Spray—for cleaning wounds, especially puncture wounds. Squeeze out generously over wound. It will help flush foreign materials and germs out of the wound. Follow with an application of non-alcohol based herbal tincture of Golden Seal or Echinacea.

1/2 oz Bottle of Golden seal Tincture in a non-alcohol base—for disinfecting wounds. Squeeze at least one dropper full of non-alcoholic tincture over the affected area. It will also help alleviate gingivitis if swabbed onto the dog's gums with a cotton swab. DO NOT USE THIS TINCTURE IN YOUR DOG'S MOUTH FOR MORE THAN 10 DAYS IN A ROW.

Note: NEVER APPLY AN ALCOHOL BASED TINCTURE TO AN OPEN WOUND. IT WILL CAUSE THE WOUND TO BURN AND INCREASE YOUR DOGS PAIN.

½ oz powdered Turkey Rhubarb—to stop bleeding of minor wounds. Make sure your hands and the dog's wound are

clean and then simply sprinkle a generous amount of the powdered herb over the wound. Not recommended for large or puncture wounds.

1 Bag of Red Raspberry Leaf Tea—for relief of minor irritations of the eye.

1 Bag of Bergamot Tea—for irrigating ears to avoid ear infections.

Two 1oz dropper bottles—for administering medicinal teas or tinctures to your dog.

2 paper coffee filters—to strain the eye and ear wash prior to use.

Additional Items to Keep on Hand for Dogs in an Emergency

Ascriptin— **For dogs larger than 35 pounds it's okay to administer Ascriptin. This over-the- counter pain reliever is a blend of aspirin and Maalox. Each tablet is meant for a person or dog weighing 75 pounds.**

A dog weighing 35 to 70 pounds should be given ½ a tablet up to 3 times daily. A dog weighting 75 to 90 pounds can be given 1 whole tablet up to 3 times daily. A giant breed dog weighing 90+ pounds can be given 2 whole tablets up to 3 times daily. Administer the Ascriptin at least 4 hours apart as needed.

Warning for cats: DO NOT GIVE ASCRIPTIN TO A CAT. IT WILL DIE IF YOU DO.

Warning for dogs: DO NOT USE ASCRIPTIN ON A DOG WEIGHING LESS THAN 35

POUNDS. IT'S TOO DIFFICULT TO GET THE DOSAGE LOW ENOUGH.

DO NOT GIVE ASCRIPTIN TO A DOG WHO IS BLEEDING OR HAS BLOODY STOOL. IT WILL MAKE THE BLEEDING WORSE.

DO NOT GIVE REGULAR ASPIRIN TO A DOG. IT WILL CAUSE STOMACH UPSET.

CBG Extract—for relief of ear infection. It contains Chickweed, Black Cohosh and Golden Seal. *Available through Nature's Sunshine Products

Aloe Vera gel—for burns

Milk Thistle—in case of poisoning

Non-alcohol based Mullein tincture—for relief of ear pain and cough 1 Two oz ear bulb—to administer ear wash to larger dogs.

Note: If at all possible, try to improve your companion's diet first. Herbal remedies are meant to augment a healthy life style, not just compensate for bad habits.

Allergies

As with people, most of an animal's immunity to illness comes from the digestive system. Allergies are considered a dysfunction of the immune system. What you want to do is calm the immune system down and improve your companion's digestion.

First, if you know what your companion is allergic to, try to help your pet avoid it. Then try to put your pet on as natural a diet as she/he will tolerate. Next you'll want to supplement that diet with Acidophilus—a probiotic that helps carnivores digest proteins. You may also want to give your pet some essential fatty acids daily. The best source is fish oil, but olive oil will also work. Avoid giving your

cat a source that has lemon added to it. Lemon oil will kill a cat.

If your companion is allergic to grass, consider administering Nettle tincture once or twice daily. See page 16 for instructions on how to dilute tinctures.

Arthritis

From a holistic standpoint, arthritis is considered an auto-immune disease. The first thing you'll want to consider is putting your companion on as natural (raw) a diet as he will tolerate. As with allergies, what you want to do is calm the immune system down and improve your companion's digestion.

Next you'll want to supplement that diet with Acidophilus—a probiotic that helps carnivores digest proteins. You may also want give your pet some essential fatty acids daily. The best source is fish oil, but avoid using a source that has lemon added to it if you have a cat. Lemon oil will kill a cat.

Any other herbal supplement you wish to consider for your companion depends on his medical history. You'll also want to consider administering something for his pain. See page 64 for information on pain relief.

Asthma & Bronchitis

Consider administering Mullein tincture 2 to 3 times daily.

See page 16 for instructions on how to dilute tinctures.

If something stronger is needed, consider trying a product called ALJ which is produced by Nature's Sunshine Products. This liquid herbal extract is composed of Boneset, Fenugreek seeds, Horseradish root, Mullein leaves and Fennel seed and is very effective for alleviating breathing problems.

You'll need to dilute it in water as you would dilute a tincture. Be sure to keep the proportion of drops to weight the same as you would for an adult weighing 150 pounds. For this remedy a 10 pound cat shouldn't need more than 2 drops

diluted in an ounce of water. Then give her one dropper full of the dilution at a time.

Steam is also good for lung problems. You might want to have your companion in the bathroom with you when you take a shower if possible.

Bite or Puncture Wound

The goal here is to flush germs and any foreign materials out of the wound before it becomes infected. Squeeze sterile saline nasal spray over and into the wound. Your goal is to wash out the wound as much as possible. Follow with an application of non-alcohol based herbal tincture of Oregon Grape, Golden Seal or Echinacea. You may have to do this a few times a day for a few days to keep the wound clean until it heals over. If there are no signs of improvement or you notice swelling around the bite, consider

a trip to the vet.

DO NOT USE POWERED TURKEY RHUBARB ON A DEEP WOUND. IT COULD CAUSE THE WOUND TO FESTER.

Bladder Infection

First, try changing to a holistic diet. Often this is sufficient to clear up the infection. Be aware that cats need food low in magnesium to help avoid kidney problems as they mature. If changing the diet doesn't work, consider administering Cranberry tincture, 3 to 4 times daily, for a few days. If the infection persists for more than 10 days, consider taking Fluffy to the vet.

See page 16 for instructions on how to dilute tinctures.

Caution: Don't give your companion Cranberry tincture if you know she has a kidney problem.

Bleeding of a Small Wound or Cut.

On a clean wound and with clean hands, sprinkle a generous amount of powered Turkey Rhubarb over the wound. It will stick to the wound by itself. Leave it in place. If the powder gets washed out of the wound/cut it will start bleeding again. The powder will wear away as the wound heals. It shouldn't be necessary to apply a bandage unless your companion licks the wound too much to let the powder work.

Burns, Minor Only

Bathe the burn immediately with lots of cool water. Then apply Aloe Vera gel to the affected area. Avoid using too much Aloe Vera for too long. It might give your companion diarrhea.

Cancer

This is a very serious situation for both you and your companion. You as the caregiver have some very difficult decisions to make. Allopathic treatment for cancer is often very expensive and traumatic for the entire family. However, holistic alternatives do exist.

After you've both come home from the vet, the first thing you'll want to consider is putting your companion on as natural (raw) a diet as she will tolerate. This is sometimes difficult but worth a try or two. Also consider administering Cat's Claw tincture, 3 to 4 times daily. See page 16 for instructions on how to dilute tinctures.

Also check the internet for info on holistic cancer treatments for your companion. What you'll need depends on the type of cancer your pet has.

If you decide to put your companion to sleep, that's okay too. The decision is yours.

Constipation

Try giving your companion a teaspoon full of fish oil in their food. DO NOT GIVE YOUR CAT FISH OIL WITH LEMON ADDED. Lemon oil will kill a cat.

You might alternatively use olive oil or butter.

Cough

What one uses to help alleviate a cough depends on why one has a cough.

If the cough is related to asthma, bronchitis or a cold, try Mullein tincture 2 to 3 times daily.

If something stronger is needed, Nature's Sunshine Products produces ALJ, a liquid herbal extract composed of Boneset, Fenugreek seeds, Horseradish root, Mullein leaves and Fennel seed which is very effective for breathing problems.

Steam is also good for lung problems. Try keeping your companion in the bathroom with you when you take a shower. The steam should help.

If your companion's cough is related to cancer, consider administering Cat's Claw tincture.

See page 16 for instructions on how to dilute tinctures.

Diabetes

If you decide against allopathic treatment for your companion, consider administering Dandelion tincture once or twice daily.

Diarrhea

Adding some powered Slippery Elm to food is often affective to alleviate diarrhea. If the stool is bloody, try administering Yarrow tincture in addition to Slippery Elm. One or two doses of Yarrow are often sufficient. The probiotic, Acidophilus, is helpful too. If the diarrhea lasts for more than a week, or gets worse, consider a trip to the vet. For very small cats and kittens, a trip to the vet is needed if the remedy doesn't work within 24 hours.

Ear Infection

Based on my experience, dogs are more prone to ear infections than cats. However, I've found a simple remedy that's appropriate for both. Nature's Sunshine Products makes a liquid herbal remedy called CBG Extract. Its contents include Chickweed, Black Cohosh and Golden Seal. If you're in a hurry, you can use it on your companion straight from the bottle. Simply shake, drip a drop or two into the affected ear and massage for a while. Sometimes one dose is enough clear up the problem. But since it comes in an alcohol base, avoid using it straight from the bottle if the ear in question is sore or raw.

Ear Mites

To a one ounce dropper bottle, add:

½ Tablespoon of Olive Oil

and one dropperful of Oregon Grape Root tincture.

Set this in the sun for two hours.

Shake well add three to four drops to the

affected ear, and massage two to three times daily.

Ear Pain Drops for Cats

To 1 oz dropper bottle add:

1 tablespoon CBG Extract available from Nature's Sunshine Products

1 tablespoon olive oil

2-3 droppers full of non-alcohol based Mullein Extract

Shake well. Add a drop or 2 into the effected ear and massage.

You'll also want to irrigate your companion's ears with ear wash once or twice a week until the infection clears up. If it doesn't clear up within 2 weeks, consider a trip to the vet.

Ear Infection, Chronic

If your companion suffers from chronic ear infections, the first thing you'll want to do is switch him to as natural a diet as possible. If you've already done that, and

he's still having ear infections, the next thing you'll want to try is administering essential fatty acids daily. The best source is fish oil, but avoid using a source that has lemon added to it. Lemon oil will kill a cat.

Also consider irrigating his ears with ear wash on a regular basis.

To make ear wash: First, make Bergamot tea: Bring one cup of filtered water to a boil. Take off of the heat and add a tea bag. Let steep for 10 minutes. Allow to cool. Strain through a coffee filter to remove all particles from the liquid.

For a cat, pour a dropper full of ear wash in to each ear and rub the ear gently. Then let the cat shake his head. The ear wash should help dislodge any dirt or earwax from the ear. The ear wash will also help clean bacteria and other microbes out of the ear and help your cat avoid ear infections. Be sure to use the ear wash at room temperature. It's okay to warm the bottle up under hot running water if you've stored it in the refrigerator, but don't get the drops too hot. Test them on your wrist, as you would a

baby's bottle.

Un-refrigerated, the wash should last 7 to 10 days. If refrigerated, the ear wash should store safely for up to 6 months.

Eye Irritation-

If your companion gets something in her eyes, a quick way to help is to flush out her eyes with an herbal wash. Our dog Tatum once got into an ant's nest. The eye wash listed below cleared up her problem in one day. This wash is safe for cats too.

To make eye wash: First, make Raspberry leaf tea: Bring one cup of filtered water to a boil. Take off of the heat and add a tea bag. Let steep for 10 minutes. Allow to cool. Strain through a coffee filter to remove all particles from the liquid. Pour 1 ounce of sterile saline solution into a clean container. Add ½ tea spoon of cooled and strained Raspberry leaf tea. (Tea made from the fruit of raspberries won't work.) Shake gently to distribute

the tea throughout the saline solution. Pour into a 1 oz dropper bottle and apply a drop or two in the effected eye twice daily for a few days. The eye wash may work in only one application.

Be sure to use the drops at room temperature. It's okay to warm the bottle up under hot running water if you've stored it in the refrigerator, but don't get the drops too hot. Test them on your wrist, as you would a baby's bottle.

If the irritation persists for more than a few days, consider taking your cat to the vet.

Unrefrigerated, the drops should last 7 to 10 days. If refrigerated the eyewash should store safely for up to 6 months.

Note: Go ahead and drink the rest of the Raspberry tea, if you wish. You probably won't need to make more than one bottle of eyewash to help your cat.

Fur Ball

Try a teaspoon full of olive oil. Butter may also be helpful.

Gingivitis

First, try getting your companion to eat a natural diet, including raw bones. If that doesn't work, try dipping a cotton swab in non-alcohol based Golden Seal tincture and gently rub the swab across the involved gums. Don't use Golden Seal for more than 10 days straight. It can have a negative impact on your companion's digestive system.

Heart Failure, Congestive

If you decide against allopathic treatment for your companion, try administering a tincture of Hawthorne, which includes the leaf and berry.

See page 16 for instructions on how to dilute tinctures.

Pain

Try administering Feverfew tincture 2 to 3 times daily, as needed for pain. FEVERFEW WILL NOT HELP ALLEVEATE PAIN FOR A DOG.

How to Prepare a Tincture for a Cat: You'll need a 1 oz dropper bottle filled to the shoulder with filtered water. (Tap water will work too, if that's all you have available.) If the instructions on the bottle of tincture say, "Add 30 to 40 drops to an ounce of water," you'll need to cut the dosage down to 1 drop of tincture in the bottle per every 5 pounds of your companion's weight. Then give your companion one dropper full of the diluted tincture.

Poisoning

If you suspect your companion has been exposed to a poison, and is still conscious, try administering Milk Thistle tincture as soon as possible and go to the vet. I've had good success in mixing the tincture directly into a glob of butter

and forcing it into the animal's mouth.

See page 16 for instructions on how to dilute tinctures.

Use butter instead of water in this case.

Seizures

If you decide against allopathic treatment for your companion, try administering Skullcap tincture 2 to 3 times daily. If the seizures don't stop completely, try adding Valerian tincture to the dilution. See page 16 for instructions on how to dilute tinctures.

Stress relief

Administer 2 drops or one dropper full of diluted Rescue Remedy under your cat's tongue. Rescue Remedy is very effective for relief of emotional upset and/or minor pain. It will help keep your cat calm if administered prior

to visiting the vet and prior to grooming. It will also help comfort the dying. Rescue Remedy also comes in an alcohol-free formula, which can be administered directly from the bottle.

Trauma, Severe

If your cat is unlucky enough to get hit by a car, or suffers some other severe, life threatening injury you need to get him to a vet as soon as possible. While in transit you'll want to gently rub the tip of one of his ears. I know this sounds off beat. However, the ear is a life energy point used in the TTellington Touch system.

Recommended Supplies to Have Available In Case of Emergencies for Your Cat

Kit available from HerbalCindy.com

Alcohol-Free Rescue Remedy Administer 2 drops or one dropper full of diluted Rescue Remedy under your dogs tongue. Rescue Remedy is very effective for relief of emotional upset and/or minor pain.

Alcohol-Free Rescue Remedy can be administered directly from the bottle if necessary.

1 (5 count) Package of Slippery Elm Capsules—to help relieve diarrhea. Each capsule is meant for a person weighing 75 pounds. A cat can be given a sprinkle of the herb, in food, once or twice daily as needed.

Sterile Saline Nasal Spray—for cleaning wounds, especially puncture wounds. Squeeze out generously over wound. It will help flush foreign material and germs

out of the wound. Follow with an application of non-alcohol based herbal tincture of Golden seal or Echinacea.

1/2 oz. Bottle of Fever Few tincture—for relief of pain. Be sure to dilute as indicated on page 16 before administering to your cat.

1/2 oz Bottle of Goldenseal Tincture in a non-alcohol base—for disinfecting wounds. Squeeze at least one dropper full of Non-alcoholic tincture over the affected area. Will also help alleviate gingivitis if swabbed onto your cat's gums with a cotton swab. DO NOT USE THIS TINCTURE IN YOUR CAT'S MOUTH FOR MORE THAN 10 DAYS IN A ROW.

Note: NEVER APPLY AN ALCOHOL BASED TINCTURE TO AN OPEN WOUND. IT WILL CAUSE THE WOUND TO BURN AND INCREASE YOUR CAT'S PAIN.

½ oz powdered Turkey Rhubarb—to stop bleeding of minor wounds. Make sure your hands and the cat's wound are clean and then simply sprinkle a generous amount of the powdered herb over the wound. Not recommended for large or puncture wounds.

1 Bag of Red Raspberry Leaf Tea—for relief of minor irritations of the eye.

1 Bag of Bergamot Tea—for irrigating ears to avoid ear infections.

Two 1oz dropper bottles—for administering medicinal teas to your cat.

Two paper coffee filters—to strain the eye and ear wash prior to use.

Additional Items to Keep on Hand for Cats in an Emergency

Aloe Vera gel—for burns

Milk Thistle—in case of poisoning

Non-alcohol based Mullein tincture—for relief of ear pain and cough.

Recommended Reading

All You Ever Wanted to Know About Herbs for Pets, Mary Wulff-Tilford & Gregory L. Tilford. Bowtie Press, 1999.

The Encyclopedia of Natural Pet Care (Revised Edition), C.J. Puotinen. Keats Publishing, 2000.

Bach Flower Remedies for Animals, Helen Graham & Gregory Vlamis. Findhorn Press, 2004.

Bibliography

Bell, Kristen Leigh. ***Holistic Aromatherapy for Animals***, Forres, Scotland: Findhorn Press, 2002.

Graham, Helen & Gregory Vlamis. ***Bach Flower Remedies for Animals***, Forres, Scotland: Findhorn Press, 2004.

Jones, Larissa. ***Aromatherapy for Mind, Body, Spirit***, Salt Lake City Utah: Evergreen Aromatherapy, 2002.

Pitcairn, Richard H., D.M.V, PhD, & Susan Hubble Pitcairn. ***Dr. Pitcairn's Complete Guide to Natural Health for Dogs and Cats*** (Updated Edition), Emmaus, Pennsylvania: Rodale Press, Inc, 1995.

Poutinen, CJ, DMV. ***The Encyclopedia of Natural Pet Care*** (Revised Edition), Los Angeles: Keats Publishing, 2000.

Mary L Wulff-Tilford & Gregory L. Tilford. ***All You Ever Wanted to Know About Herbs for Pets,*** Irvin, California: Bowtie Press, 1999.

Index

About the Author

C.D. Meacham is a Master Herbalist, Natural Health Consultant, Aromatherapist, and Bach Flower Practitioner. She lives with her husband and four children (three of which are fuzzy) in Phoenix, Arizona.

To learn more about her, visit her website, www.herbalcindy.com.

www.ingramcontent.com/pod-product-compliance
Ingram Content Group UK Ltd.
Pitfield, Milton Keynes, MK11 3LW, UK
UKHW040557210726
13854UKWH00007B/1370

9 780557 695768